new names for lost things

new names for lost things

noor unnahar

Andrews McMeel
PUBLISHING®

For my baba,
Maaz Hashim Siddique.
The quiet one, who instilled calmness
& courage in me. This book is for you.

"THIS IS MY LETTER TO THE WORLD
THAT NEVER WROTE TO ME"

–Emily Dickinson

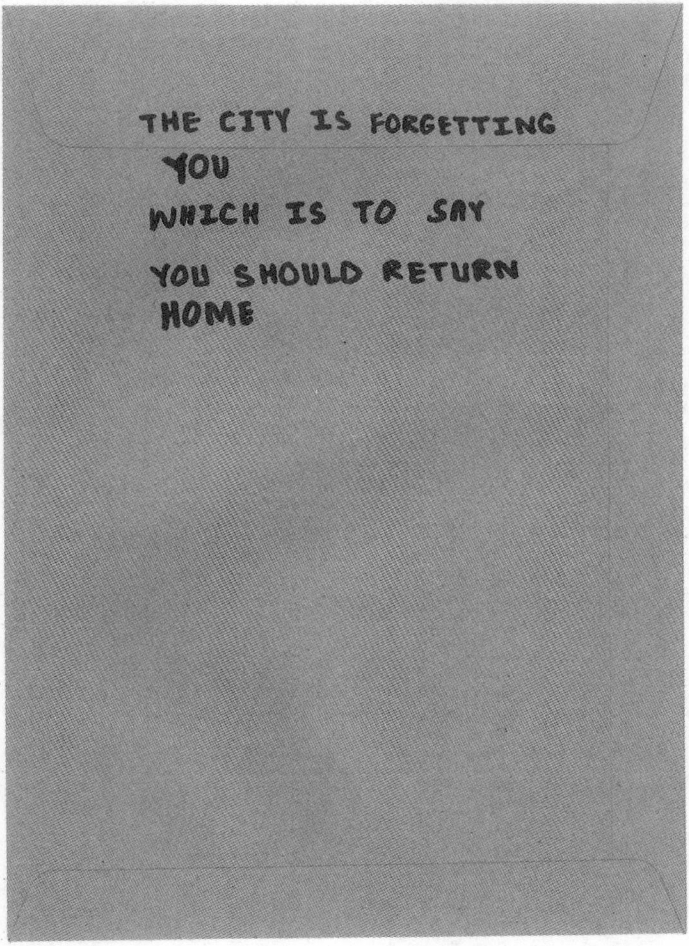
THE CITY IS FORGETTING
YOU
WHICH IS TO SAY
YOU SHOULD RETURN
HOME

[A Ghazal]

love seeks every to-be-loved   just like that
[exactly] how death cradles life until it doesn't   just like that

my mother was the middle child   my father   the aloof child
& I became their difficult child   just like that

dried mustard flowers on fire   became another source of light
when burning was   the new way to live   just like that

seven roses crushed together   on the yellow pedestrian bridge
someone has contaminated this path with heartbreak   just like that

Jupiter, January, just-forget-them   are my favorite J words
you see   my vocabulary has been upsetting   just like that

[Lucid Dreaming]

Everything I know about you, I know it from the absence of you. All the crushed glass on the road I once thought was water is coming back to me. I wash my hands and there's blood everywhere. I run the faucets and they only glow. This city has been eating its loneliness again (I thought you should know about it).

you and your popular loneliness

[Inheritance]

I inherited prayers / voice / absence from my father
& acceptance / eyes / borders from my mother
& rage / hands / justice from my grandfather
& gold / hair / confusion from my grandmother
& obsession / feet / generosity from my younger aunt
& forgetting / moles / fright from my older aunt
& music / nails / power from my uncle

The luck tastes like stale things in our family / no one gets to choose a better flavor
I have picked the taste of cold tea / every mug I forget is still the one I drink / every
gulp reminds me / about everything / where I come from

[The Origin Story]

Superstition: the eclipse leaves the celestial beings in agony.
A moon, wailing. A sun, dying. Our mothers whispering
Arabic verses to lessen their pain. But did it ever work?

Your grief knows my grief by its false name. Relief, relief.
My days are melting into answered prayers. Belief: ask, but
never twice.
There's a mirror standing still where the home is. Which is
to say, I'll have to come back to me.

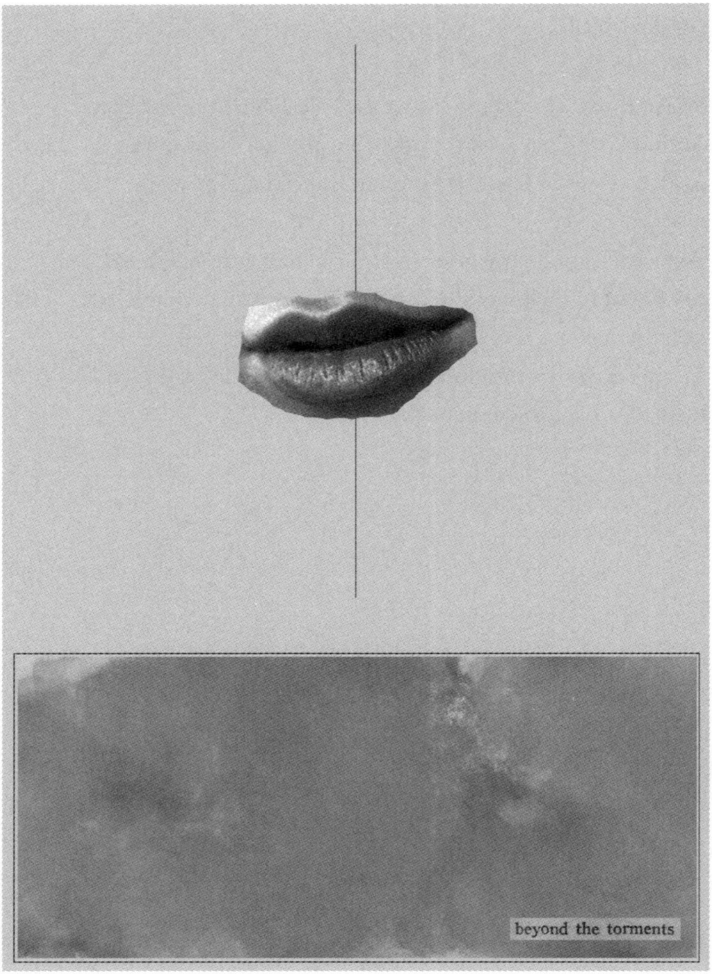
beyond the torments

[One-Sided]

I learned to say thank you in three dialects. It is your fault.
No one should leave love behind. Ever.
Where will you go with this bubblegum heart of yours?
In another universe   I am a lump of coal   You are too
The day grandma died   the sky was as pale as the apricots
she would buy   from the flea market three hours away.

The day I lost two dreams in a row   the sky was in the mood
of laughing out loud   It rained once
Have you seen my loneliness?   It lives in New York & Karachi &
Tokyo & Amsterdam   now
The last dream I had   our city's name translated to "where fish
come to yell"
Have you been   dreaming lately?

[Promises in Making]

The love you'll be given will be given from the dawn /
from the light that is born from the hunger of the sky.
The grief you'll be given / will be given from home /
from the point of origin where we all eventually go /
what we all eventually donate to the teeth of rage.
The courage you'll be given / will be given from
the dead / from the one blind eye that takes away
the rest / that never forgives things that weren't
meant to be said.

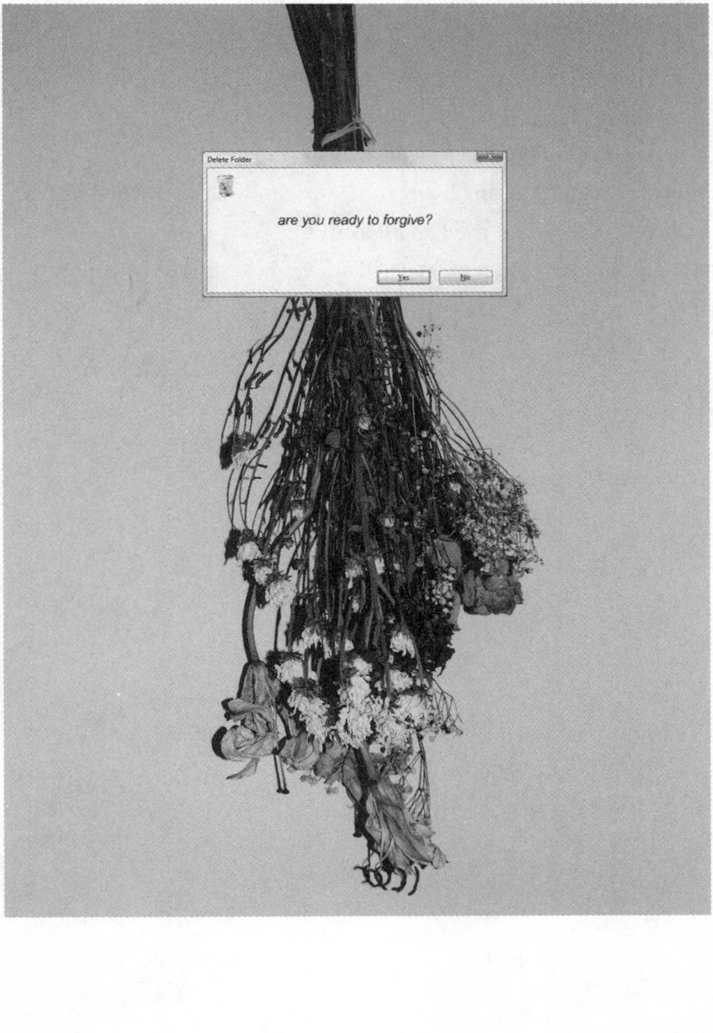
Delete Folder
are you ready to forgive?
Yes
No

[An Archived Panic]

What do you tell home before
abandoning it? You vow to return.
You reinvent a destined loneliness
before meeting it. I am ready to be forgotten, to be turned into an
archived panic. The grief of this city
has inherited my fingers. We will always have this in common.

[A Personal Tragedy]

This unstitched loneliness keeps bleeding out of my hands. I was always ready to be someone else. To be remembered like a fabricated war history. Reunion with myself remains a personal tragedy. But to be a poet without being tragic would have been quite a shame.

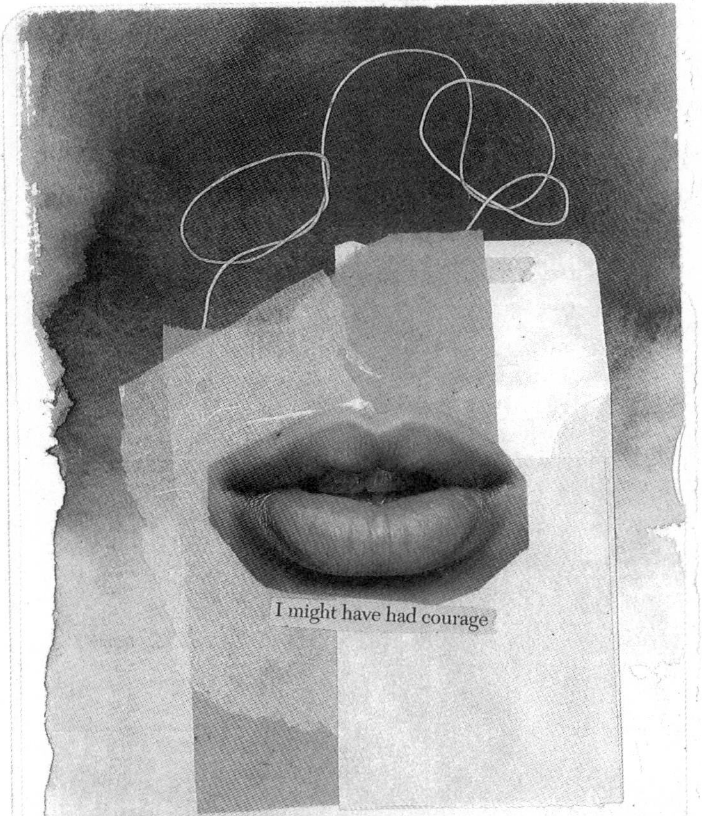
I might have had courage

[Dawning]

You were so protected once—
it almost made you ungrateful. Look what
safety does to bodies reliant on it. I could
have been something else. A cobalt sparrow
on a withering tree. A fragile pearl on a cashmere coat.
An unnamed star adjacent to the moon. But I was given
this life. Too many wants stitched inside
a warm blood house. I could have left it
behind. But I was given this time.

[The Secret Life of Longing]

Longing has a pretty face. She
lives in a rented cottage. She says absence when she means to
say disguise.
She delivers the mail of loneliness. She never leaves the
house without counting her ribs. She is only alive to see one
of us die.

[DESCRIBE YOURSELF IN A POEM]

I AM
DAYLIGHT SOLIDIFIED/ MY ANXIOUS
FATHER'S ABSOLUTE FAVORITE CHILD/
GLADLY TERRIBLE AT LOVE/ DECADES
AWAY FROM HOME / REPEATER OF
BAD SAD SONGS/ THE SOBER DRIVER
ON THE WRONG LANE / AN EAGER
ENEMY OF MOSQUITOES/ YESTERDAY'S
FULL MOON / THE EPIGRAPH OF
A LONELY BOOK/ A CHEF NOT TO
BE TRUSTED/ THE REMAINDER OF
A FAMILY ON FIRE/ A NEON
DANGER SIGN / & A HEARTACHE
SEVERAL WATER BODIES AWAY

[Verdict]

your hands can no longer shelter history / they turned into maps
ages ago / i am moonless again / the last time i saw the light /
she was pleading with the god / just like the rest of us

[A Questionnaire]

It's fairly simple. My misery
is childlike. It forgets its name. ( ) But never
where it came from.
Did you see how loneliness shrouds everything that isn't held?
How do you forgive an injured light? How do you let go of a grief
that was never born?

Extremely dark or gloomy;

[A Tired Confession]

good god,
my guilt has three faces &
none of them was born with eyes.
why does a heart inherit a cage
but no key to keep it there?
I will drown if my anger asks me to.
it has an ocean to its name. it has
everything I wasn't given.

[A Decision]

tell me / what city promised you
a lifetime of remembrance? / they forget by the hour / 24 times
a day /
last night / someone said distance /
& i mistook it for your name

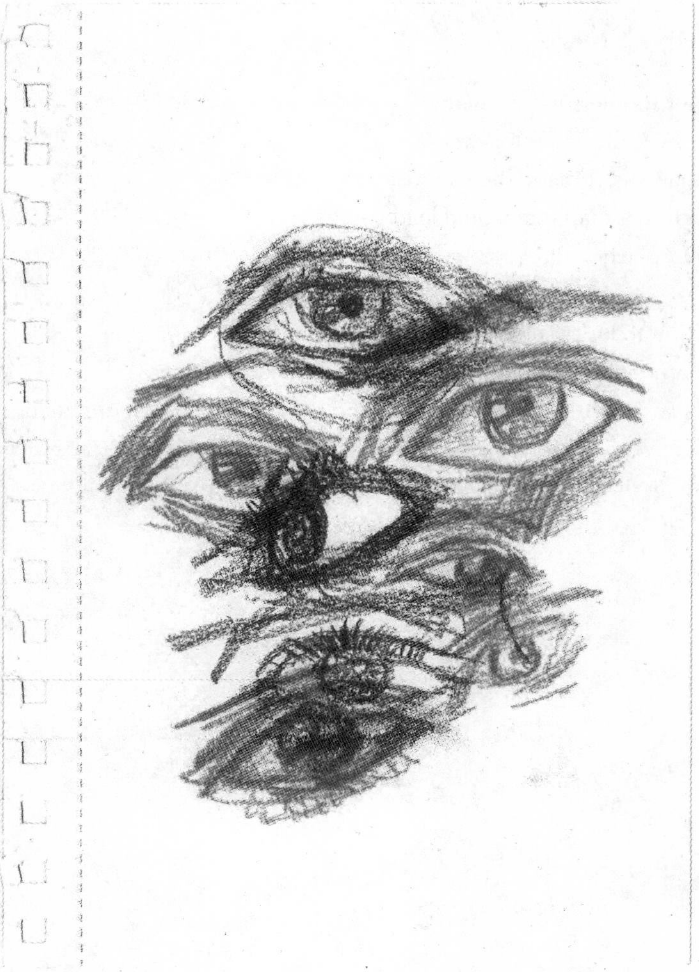

[A Reluctant Heir]

our mothers left us their
eyes & their love for everything
that wasn't made theirs. i mean my
skin is a map that would lead you to
her & when did i agree to that?

i wanted to reverse the damage my
name inherited / but is it possible / i mean
how do you devour silence without wrecking it / without making
it a weapon / our mothers left us their grief & their love for every-
thing that brought it / when did you agree to that?

[In Line of Duty]

Summon your quiet loneliness. Summon the wretched
grief that gave birth to your heart. Summon the moon of
your origin. Summon the love poem your quill slaughtered.
Summon the war and its children.
(Which is to say, summon everything that will protect your
beloved.)
You have never been sheltered. You must never repeat what
history left in you.

[A CONVERSATION WITH A
TIRED MOON]

SOME TRAGEDIES HAVE NAMES,
SOME ONLY HAVE BODIES

I LOOKED AT HIM
& DIDN'T SEE MY
FATHER; HE LOOKED
IN THE MIRROR &
DIDN'T SEE HIS FATHER

TOGETHER WE TORE THE SUN,
IT WAS COLD INSIDE
& LEFT MY HEART, IT
SPOKE OF RUSTY HOPE INSIDE

[Opening of a Window]

Ask the sky about absence
& it will show you my palms
Look, it was either a home or
a sharpened knife of freedom & I chose what
was to rip my heart open first
I am alive but at what cost / Is that because
someone was listening / Or is it because
no one was

[Afterword]

On days like this,
home becomes a wound
to weep into. I have nothing
left to name. Everything that
remembers you—has
forgotten me. Just like that.
Just like that.

the long way home

[A Confession of an Artist]

it's of no use / this gruesome joy /
it is bound to turn my art stagnant / it is
bound to evacuate its only
driving force / a lifetime of grief

[Renaissance]

Everything in this world was
once nothing. The beauty, too, was
birthed by nameless holy bodies. I
would have liked to see it happen.
How the sky acquired its monumental loneliness.
How our grief never learned a new language. But I wasn't there.

I would like to see my life bloom
into a beguiling thing. A simple act of renaissance.

It has happened before. You weren't
there to see it.

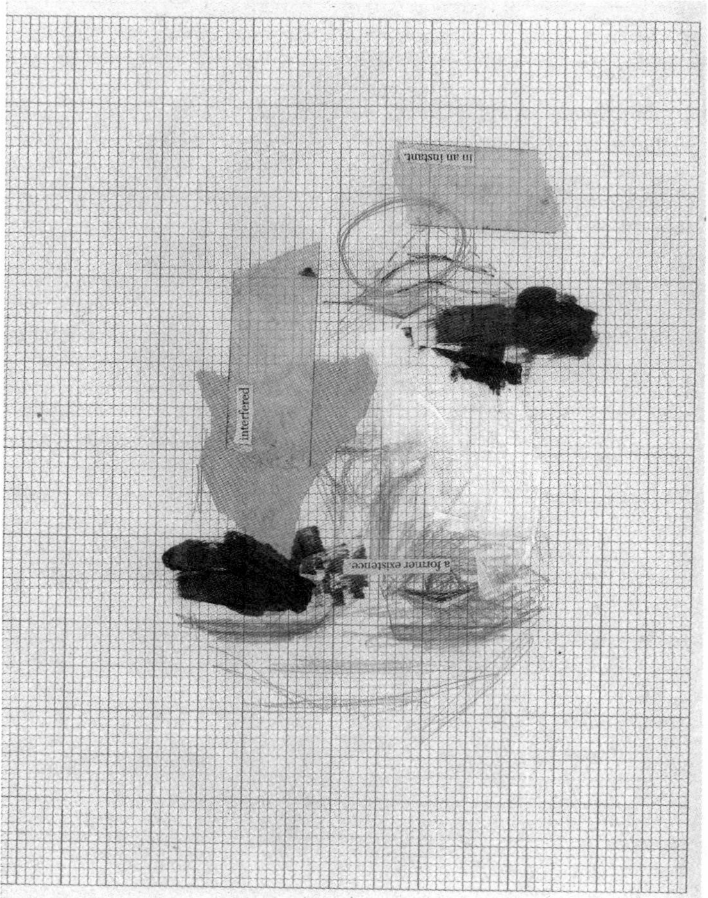
in an instant,
interfered
a former existence.

[The Hunted]

You wanted to say (safety) and it came out (abandoned). Our cities have forgotten all of their promises. Like when the sun sets, it mustn't set into a corpse. Like when the moon comes out, it should do so without a bullet in it.

[A Request]

but if the hour finds my heart
with only half of its teeth
will you rescue it with the silence
that is only holy and astonished
I have been taught how to be left behind
frequently and entirely empty-handed

[TRAVELERS]

A TWILIGHT TRAPPED BETWEEN MY
LUCK AND YOURS
I CHECK EVERY WINDOW HIDING FAMILIAR LIGHTS
TO HAVE A GLIMPSE OF HOME
BEFORE THE SUNSET
TO IMAGINE OUR WALLS' CHIPPING WHITES
NEVER ASK A TRAVELER ABOUT
THE WARMTH OF HOME
AND EVERYTHING ELSE THEY LEFT BEHIND

FOR SOME, THE ROAD'S A
REGAL
ABODE

FOR SOME, A HOME THEY WOULD NEVER
FIND

[Patience]

Your home fits into a name & that is a reward. Let's say
the rage in you was nothing
but a lifetime of grief boiled
enough. Whoever named you after the sea forgot about the
hurricanes. It was never about the patience—it was always
about when it ran out.

[An Invitation]

Come home before our moon starts wailing your name

Come home before the future forgets where to place you

Come home before this loneliness finds my skin to chew on

Come home before another river forgets its way

Come home before I am left empty-handed

Come home before that is the only thing to do

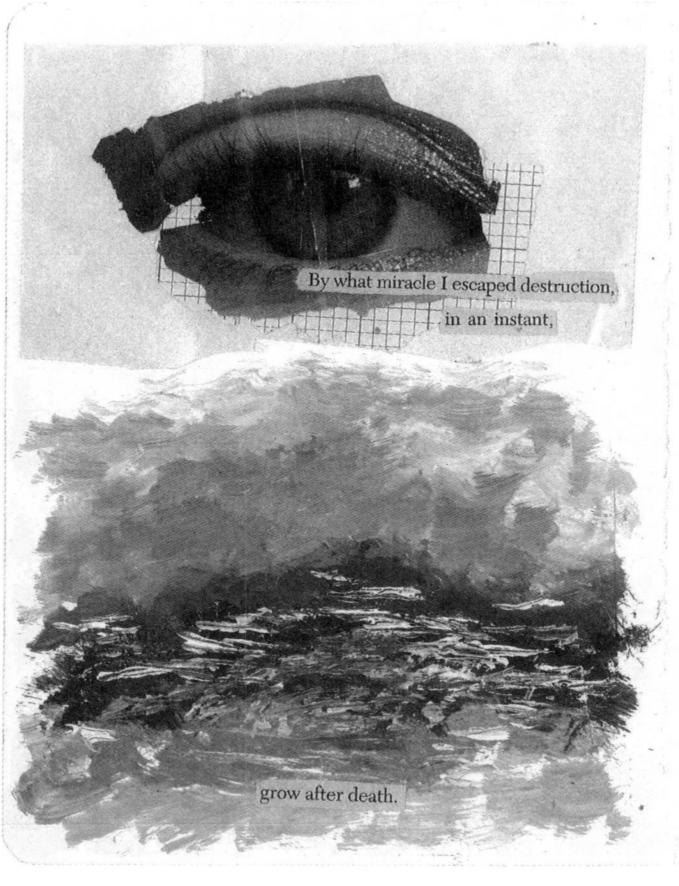
By what miracle I escaped destruction,
in an instant,
grow after death.

[From My Forgetfulness]

My grief knew exactly who I was. It
was half of who I was.

(A body with only a first name and nothing else is easily forgotten.)

My forgetfulness kept me protected
but the thing about safety is
it can't be trusted.

The art remembers everything
the artist left behind.

Even the prayers. Even the blood.

[What Else Should I Remember If Not This?]

- you were once protected by everything that wants to end you now.
- you inherited his toenails instead of his fear.
- love doesn't like your overspending.
- somewhere someone is naming their daughter after the goddess of war.
- your house will keep the sunlight alive for you.

born a daughter
a
dazzling
sound,
born a daughter
dazzling

[Remembering the Daughters]

The daughters you forget remember.
That is the part that comes with not being a son.
The daughters you forget create.
That is the part that comes with loneliness.

Daughters with sapphire eyes / daughters with desert for skin / daughters scratching the moons off the floorboards / daughters counting what remains of them

Remember.

[My Mother Asks about Love]

I want to tell you that love means I will be protected / means what love is if not sheltering / amma, it means I am seen / means what love is if not present / ma, it means I have a home address that breathes / means what love is if not within

[The Ghost House Speaks for the First Time]

The history remembers the color of your blood. & it will ask for
it once again. The family name was only there because no other
map could bring you back.
The children of the ghost house go everywhere. They have arms
wrapped around houses that will never be theirs. Their tongues
are heavy with drowned languages. Their eyes are laced with
beauty and salt.
The kids of the ghost house always return
because
no other house will ever hurt enough. No other house will ever
keep all the ghosts tied together.

[My Father Asks What Time It Is]

It is the hour when fear gets new hands. They have no memory of strangulation. It works for most people.

It is the minute when a daughter is too sure. The heart is a lawless land. The history comes here to count its days. Yes baba, it dies here.

It is the second when the moon becomes the center of this room. We are going to inhale all the poetry that has lived here. Our eyes will shed it later.

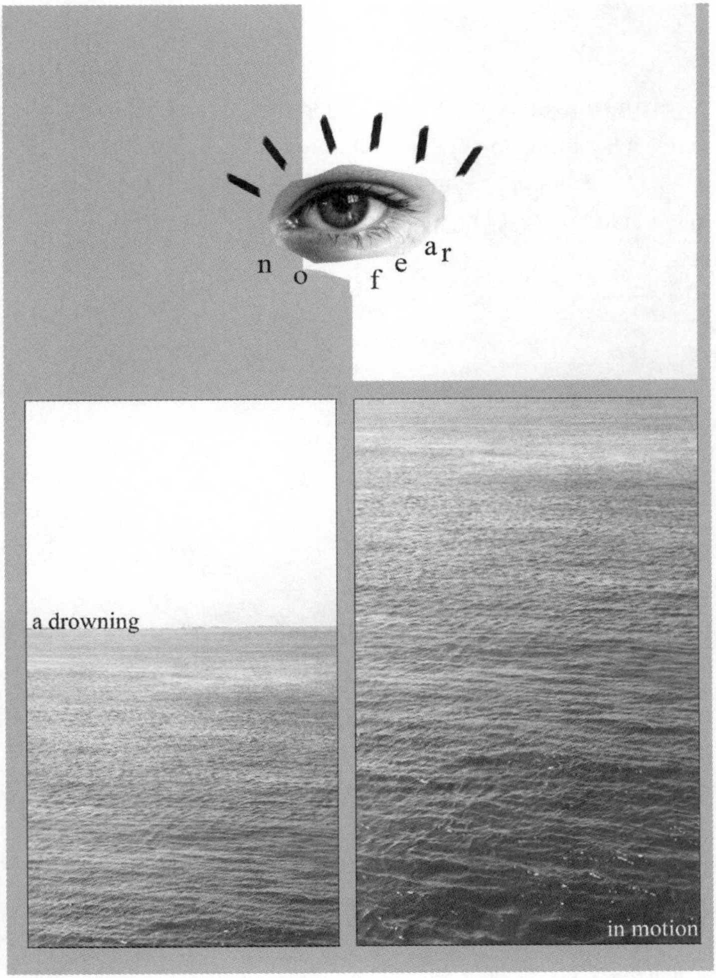
no fear
a drowning
in motion

[A Lonely Job]

An artist empty-handed is an artist too present / creation is a lonely job / in my dreams I crush stars with my teeth / their deaths have illuminated my prayers / every holy whisper turned into a gold body / I'm scared of abundance / even of love / even of loss

[Lost Things with New Names]

My memory is unwilling to rescue your memory. When the hurt found its way to the stars, it turned into the brightest names. Someday, you will look for a language but will find only a scream instead. Take the sound home and turn it into everything you were not given.

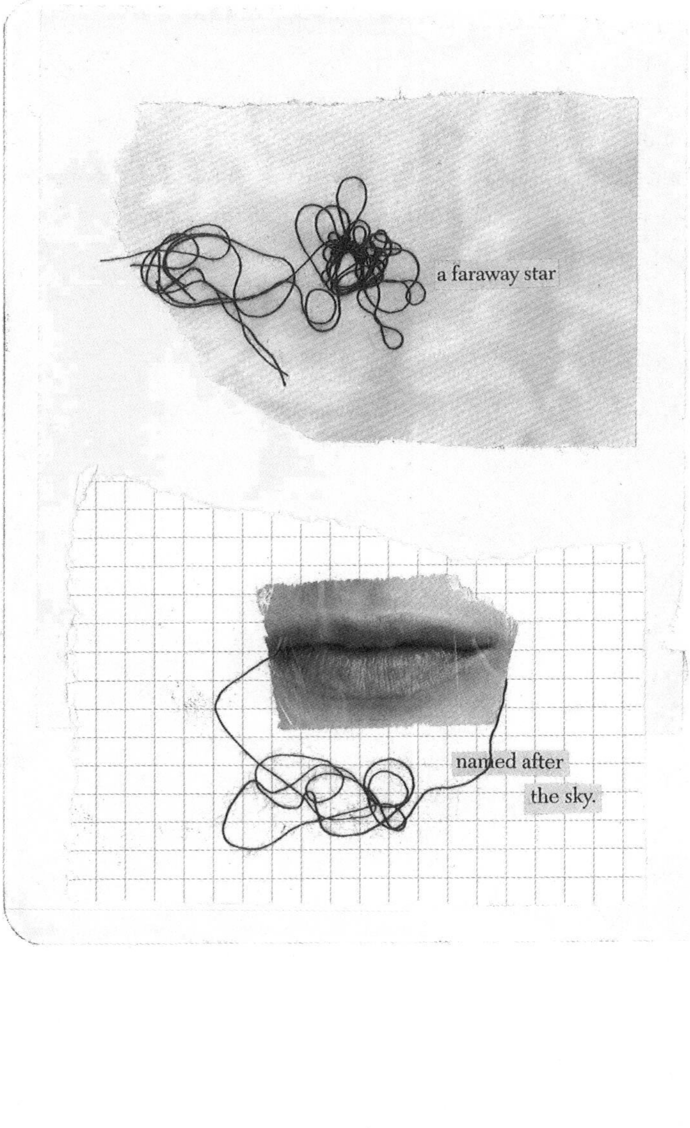
a faraway star
named after
the sky.

[Reverse]

Here is what I want to remember: reverse is a beautiful motion. Bringing a body back to its origin point. The same way death returns a body where it came from. Old dust to the new dust. My wants are becoming un-wants. Here is what I want to remember: reverse is a motion that brings everything back—except the dead.

[Pockets]

My sister insists on buying clothes with pockets. A floral kurti with pockets. An oversized shirt with pockets. An overpriced kameez with pockets.
I keep myself at a distance from them. I do not want more places to keep things. All of my belongings are safely packed. Everything neatly placed where it should be. Grief—locked in the heart. Softness—rolled under this tongue. Anger—locked away in an unnamed vein.
A pocket will come hungry. It will ask to be filled. I will put my phone in it. I will put some silver coins. I will put your absence in it & carry it everywhere. Again.

The thing about space is—it always finds something to fill itself. Yellowing yesterdays. Dying daylight. Troubled tomorrows. Even if they stay. Even if they go.

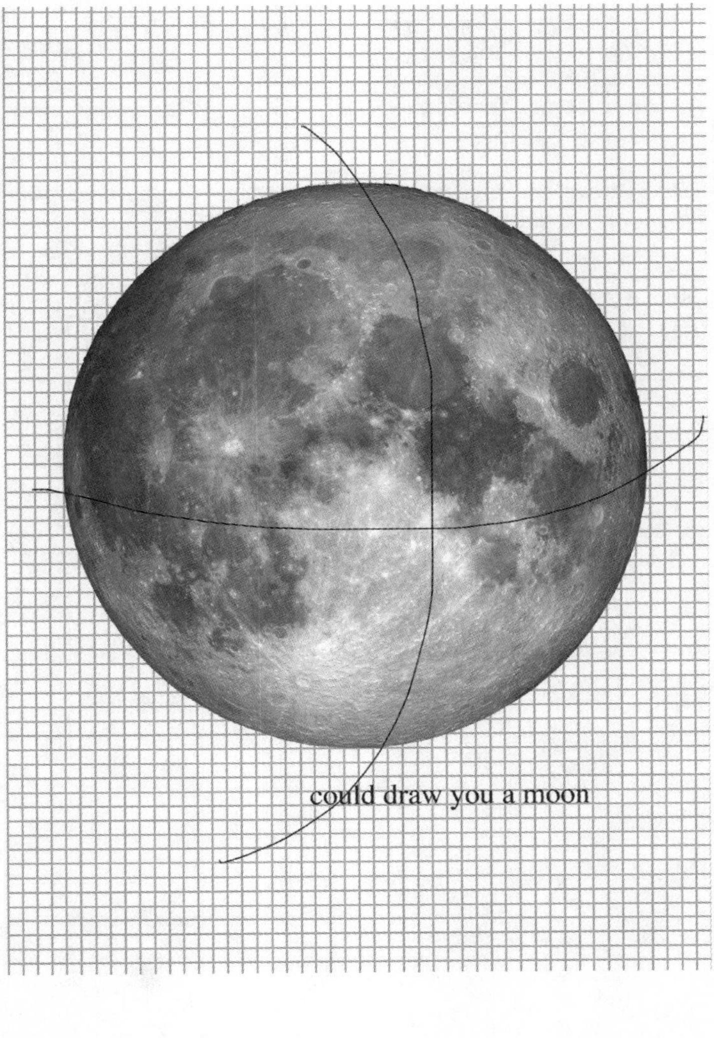
could draw you a moon

[A Timeline of Disarranged Sorrow]

Wherever the tomorrow is,
it's already a yesterday
somewhere else.
Whenever our waters fall in love with
the sinking ships,
some of us have to drown to live.
Whoever asks about the death of starts,
we tell them about the birth of
ends.

[Everyday]

I am grateful for everyone who had power but didn't exercise on me
& it's a blessing to count things without keeping them
The singularity of the Moon / every Holy prayer / the sadness of the morning sky
[ ] remember: nothing is ever lost. It pauses. It breathes. It returns.
I am learning to pay for everything even if I don't have to.
Scream for a scream. Word for a word. Forgiveness for forgiveness.
I am lost. I am pausing. I am breathing. I am returning.

LOOK AT ME. LOOK AT ME TWICE.
LOOK AT ME. LOOK AT ME TWICE.

[3 Ways to Proclaim My Mother Is a Strong Woman]

1. My mother prays for every broken thing: cities, daughters, homes, the cracked screen of my phone.
2. Nothing leaves her house unforgiven. The bodies, the language, the ache.
3. Look at me. Look at me twice.

[Language as an Identity]

I [want to] write   about magnificent things
so I [try to] narrate   stories of women &
of woe   and of men
Every -ing means there's life   a verb [body] in motion
All of the gones   become go-ing   as if you are [still] here
present like all of my fears   buried but breathing
[Here] language comes   like forgiveness   uninvited & adored
It is [cotton] soft   when my mother prays   in Arabic and Urdu
It slips [oil]   when my father is talking   to his [dying] father
Some nights   I would write   my name on a paper & drown it
This way what water takes   is [death] language
What it doesn't   is the rest [of me]

You will have to find me

[I Am Forgetting or Half-Forgiving]

Listen,
To forget is to half-forgive
Who unearths the dead to announce "you're not alive to me anymore"—they will never be not-dead

Listen,
Suppose this body is a nameless skeleton of water—coming from all the wrong directions. Suppose it has forgotten its origin—or half-forgiven it. Suppose now it is seventy percent more important than the rest of your bodies.

Listen,
We have been the moons in foreign skies. So dream of snows and emeralds. Knead the flour badly. Braid your hair into loose knots. Scratch the daylight off your walls. Water all of your dead plants and dried flowers and withering dreams. Be the thing you were named after.

[A List of Words That Are Shapeshifters]

Home / means the warm seat of your father's old car / means a room with sunlight and no furniture / means everything has ended

Love / means to be forgiven, forgiven and forgiven / means your favorite color is remembered / means you left but didn't really

Name / means you were brought to life / means there is a chance / means you reminded someone of daylight

"And how is this to be done?"
the ruin

[A List of Words That Are Shapeshifters: Part II]

Failure / means a body moved before crashing / means a tiny prayer lost its abode / means whoever carried it—is now tired

Distance / means you're here / means another way to spell your name / means I lost you to it

Memory / means nothing ever dies / means my grandmother is still alive here / means everything I left behind is still breathing

[Rebellion as One-Way Ticket]

I was a decade away
from the house of my father's
father; a sky floating in foreign orbits.
In every room of my
family home, a morning twice
my name entered. & stayed.
Outside, we were growing up
much like the polite emptiness
inside—never to stop.
Or so it seemed. Every twilight
led us to bright bodies
laughing in languages we
longed to understand. Perhaps
it was only a moon flowing in
reverse direction. Like Turkey's
rebel river Asi. Like the weight of
the shadow of my own body.

tamed

[Winters Named after My Mother]

**In Pakistan, it is widely believed that if you name someone after a person, the former party will inherit qualities of the latter party.*

Seasons were never nameless in our household / Giving them names—dainty pieces of our grace—was a mercy plea in advance / the epitome of surrender / to never despise / what's now a part of us

Every year I named winter after my mother / tore her name like a whisper and gulped / as winds sharpened their blades to invade our homes / murmuring Bismillah / followed by Surah Al-Ikhlas

I was born when summer was still in its youth / before the winter ever knew glory /
To ever love a season unfamiliar with burning / was to be an ephemeral ego /
a Sapphire crushed to death

Naming winters after a life that started mine / has always been my frail attempt / to adore a season too foreign / for bodies arising from flames / the ones who lived before their first summer died

[Tonight I Will Have an Easy Name for Dinner]

Difficult names are foreign objects floating in the air. If you ever
get struck by one, remember, remember, remember.
I wonder about the muezzin who whispered Noor Unnahar
into my uncle's ear who whispered it in a room
full of women who whispered it to the air
guarding my mother who whispered it in my ear;
making me a daughter named after light; of a mother
who was named after the sun. A name with a history
and multiple syllables is a dangerous responsibility.
Tonight, I could be a difficult name or an easy conversation
and I flip the menu until every foreign dish disappears
where each name disintegrates into an ephemeral reminder of
my crepuscular language. So tonight, I will have an easy
name for dinner, the one easier to consume
for every tongue at the table.

invite chaos invite chaos invite chaos invite chaos invite chaos invite chaos
invite chaos invite chaos invite chaos invite chaos invite chaos invite chaos
invite chaos invite chaos invite chaos invite chaos invite chaos invite chaos
invite chaos invite chaos invite chaos invite chaos invite chaos invite chaos
invite chaos invite chaos invite chaos invite chaos invite chaos invite chaos
invite chaos invite chaos invite chaos invite chaos invite chaos invite chaos
invite chaos invite chaos invite chaos invite chaos invite chaos invite chaos
invite chaos invite chaos invite chaos invite chaos invite chaos invite chaos
invite chaos invite chaos invite chaos invite chaos invite chaos invite chaos
invite chaos invite chaos invite chaos invite chaos invite chaos invite chaos
invite chaos invite chaos invite chaos invite chaos invite chaos invite chaos
invite chaos invite chaos invite chaos invite chaos invite chaos invite chaos
invite chaos invite chaos invite chaos invite chaos invite chaos invite chaos
invite chaos invite chaos invite chaos invite chaos invite chaos invite chaos
invite chaos invite chaos invite chaos invite chaos invite chaos invite chaos

[Omens in the History of My Family]

Spilled salt on a tired marble
floor was a bad omen in our
household protected
by the pleas of women in the language of
God. I was running out of luck but
forgot to say Astaghfirullah at the
sight of the ashen luck of salt. To be young
was to have the privilege of denial. My mother

fed every uninvited crow sitting
on the walls of her house
to secure her floating daughters' fates. My
late grandmother wouldn't let

boiling milk escape its pan
to keep her falling family prosperous. Our mothers
learned to fight the unseen. Their battle of faith
wasn't to redeem a victory; only for the safety of
what meant the most.
I flinch at every sight of crows
assuming they'll peck at my luck if they're hungry
and never put the milk on raging stoves
in case it burns what is left of my family along with it.

[A Detailed Answer to All of Your What's Ups]

I was so afraid / I ran into the lights / I ran into everything that was after my life / hello the good thing is / it isn't over / the dried flowers over the head of my bed / were once a gift / now they're a reminder / every body of beauty / shifts its shapes / love it while you can / love it before it goes back / dandy flowers shrinking dead / & there is no after story. I am alive while I am. There is too much future in my room. My mother thinks of me as another sun in the sky. She is even sure I have a moon of my own.

[PROSE POEM AS DISAPPOINTING SPEECH]

YOU SEE, WE WAITED FOR A GHOST TO ACQUIRE A BODY. IT ONLY ACQUIRED BAD TASTE INSTEAD. MY NAME MEANT LIGHT AND YESTERDAY EARLY-MORNING -SUNSHINE GOT TANGLED IN MY ANGRY CURLS. SO WAS LIGHT MEETING THE TANGIBLE BODY CALLED LIGHT OR ARE WE MAKING THINGS UP HERE? SCREAM AUBERGINE. SCREAM YOGURT WITH NO SUGAR. SCREAM HE WILL NEVER BE YOUR FATHER. SCREAM LONELINESS. SCREAM BURNED POTATOES. SHE SAID YOU WERE NOT MEANT TO LIVE OR WRITE BUT HERE WE ARE. IN A PARALLEL UNIVERSE, I AM A SEASON WITH PLENTY OF DAMAGING RAIN BUT HERE I CANNOT GET PAST BEING A LONELY WINTER. WHAT WAS DESERT BEFORE THE HEAT BECAME ITS MOTHER?

[Trash Kid's Song to a City with a Conceited Summer]

I stepped out of 1997 to a summer twice my age / Together we have floated over a city never kind enough / I left with a bag packed with three poems and a name

There / Our voices will always be an urban trauma / Your love will always be a season gone wrong / Always—not a word but a sword / That wouldn't ever see blood

My apologies! / Your ache cannot be of gold there / Forever an uninvited guest / This city doesn't carry hand-me-down devastation / Unlike you / Unlike us

Remind me of this city / Of its violent kind of kindness / When the rest of us are stepping out of summer / To a season thrice my age

[Arrival of Love]

Tell me, how do I contain / a joy bigger than me / —even my grief is now looking / for a different place to be.

I am trying
to fix this

[An Abandoned To-Do List]

I lived to see you die.
I lived because I knew you'd be dying.
The house isn't there / the house was never there but I was.
The ghosts in some dreams dance.
My power was that I could build me a city. I could bury you a hundred times. I could light up the sky with one star. I could name everything that was left without one. I could kill my fate with bare hands. My power was that I could write you into being. I could scream you into a void and a body would appear. Which is to say, I could summon you with a tiny breath.

[Take the light] I have saved four hundred days' worth of it, to build a heart with it.
The grief was made mine and I will forget it. Your shame will swallow you, there's no denying that.

[Home and Its Alternative Addresses]

Home—my father's family name stacked enough times to be mistaken for a building. I am light entering the memory entering the loneliness in a blind eye. (i) A withering mango tree as home because that is a thing someone once abandoned. (ii) A dried pot of paint as home because half of me is only alive when identified as an artist. (iii) A car as home because some of us only learned moving forward from a stationary body.

[Eyes of the Present]

What I am today is everything the Future will forget
I could make things happen but I counted stars instead
The Past has a razor in its decaying hands srrp srrp
it slices my memory in h a l f in h a l f
I will beg forgiveness from the lonely Present
before it grows a pair of eyes & sees how I am burning it alive

~~silence~~

~~silence~~

[Alter Ego: An Artist at Work]

Do the unholy work of remembering, which is to say, create
create / create / create

The origin of art was always the end of self. Did you find it?
What I am really asking is did you end yourself? The work is
about to begin.

The dawn comes with all of its selfish colors. Be a witness.
If the home awaits, let it know you're not coming.
Take a name to drown it. Call it a revolution. The hands have
a memory of their own. But they will forgive you.

Write the blessings for the unblessed bodies. Everything awaits.

[Athena]

The last museum I went to
housed an ancient head of the
goddess of war. Born from the forehead
of her father. I took her name and gave
it to my daughter. There's a slight chance
she will put on a helmet one day & hold
a spear. She will summon the memory
to her uncombed hair. She will sketch
a body out of a whisper. She will turn a
sidewalk into a nation. The goddess of
war was also the goddess of wisdom.
To Athena I will say: forget the
war—build the city.

there was
a way out

[Love Letter]

I think of you as a dagger without a resting place / too sharp too dangerous too exquisite to be away from home / to be away / the seas have mastered the killings / the sky can now fall / nothing says welcome without a threat

[A Poet's Heart]

My great-grandfather was also a poet. The words skipped two generations to reach me.
A poet's heart is a populous grave. Bodies turned stories turned guilt turned into a mouth. I am trying to be lonely again.

Now that I am noticing, you've been inside all of these poems.
You've been all of these poems.
A poet's heart is a populous grave. Who buried you there?

running
calm

[An Artist Not Making Art]

An artist not making art is chewing a death.
An artist not making art is a rusty knife.
An artist not making art is a starving city.
An artist not making art is a collapsing ceiling.
An artist not making art is a gulping loneliness.
An artist not making art is a wounded ocean.
An artist not making art is an empty gaze.
An artist not making art is a withering bloodroot.
An artist not making art is a desperate weapon.
An artist not making art is forgetting the way home again.

[Borrowed Luck]

My family is part superstitious part clueless. They knew I borrowed my father's luck when I entered the world. I still think I only got the driving skills.
The mauve sky meets my dreams halfway.

I name everything that is to be mine. Our last name for the birds. A lost anklet called aquamarine. An untitled departure. I've learned to rob leavings of their identities. I only name things that will stay mine.

A borrowed luck runs out faster than usual.

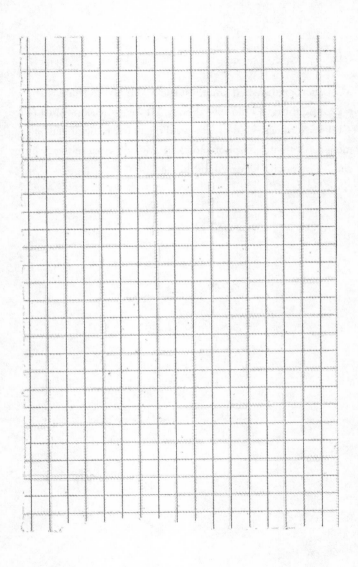

[Repetition]

My beliefs are crushed amethyst rocks / in an alternate reality / repeating things would save them / I'd wear the same shirt twice / I'd say forgiveness in my sleep / I'd call my father / half of me is a poet with anaphora stuck in my nails / there's very little chance of saving / everything I love

[Days Half Remembered]

Grief is a clock turned into a cloud turned into a ruin at the outskirts of my memory / what lessons did I learn after staying alive for this long / probably none / probably one / I can hold all goodbyes in a clenched fist / I can hold what is to leave my heart / yes, like that / so much of you resides in my forgetfulness / one day our moon will eclipse in a sky far from this city / & I will not be there to see it

I could remember,

[Family History]

Long before the August that brought us / there was always my father's December / start of summer meant I stayed alive another year / end of winter meant my father did too / to be born in my family / is to bear a responsibility / all of us are named after bright beautiful blessed things / I am their light / my sister is their wisdom / my father is their bravery / in my dreams / my luck is running out / in my present / I am carrying what remains of it

[Origin of Loneliness]

Baba would ask / where is this loneliness coming from? / and I would say / wrapped in linen / it's coming from home / humming with the light / it's coming from a moon / soaked in distance / it's coming from love / threatened by sadness / it's coming from us

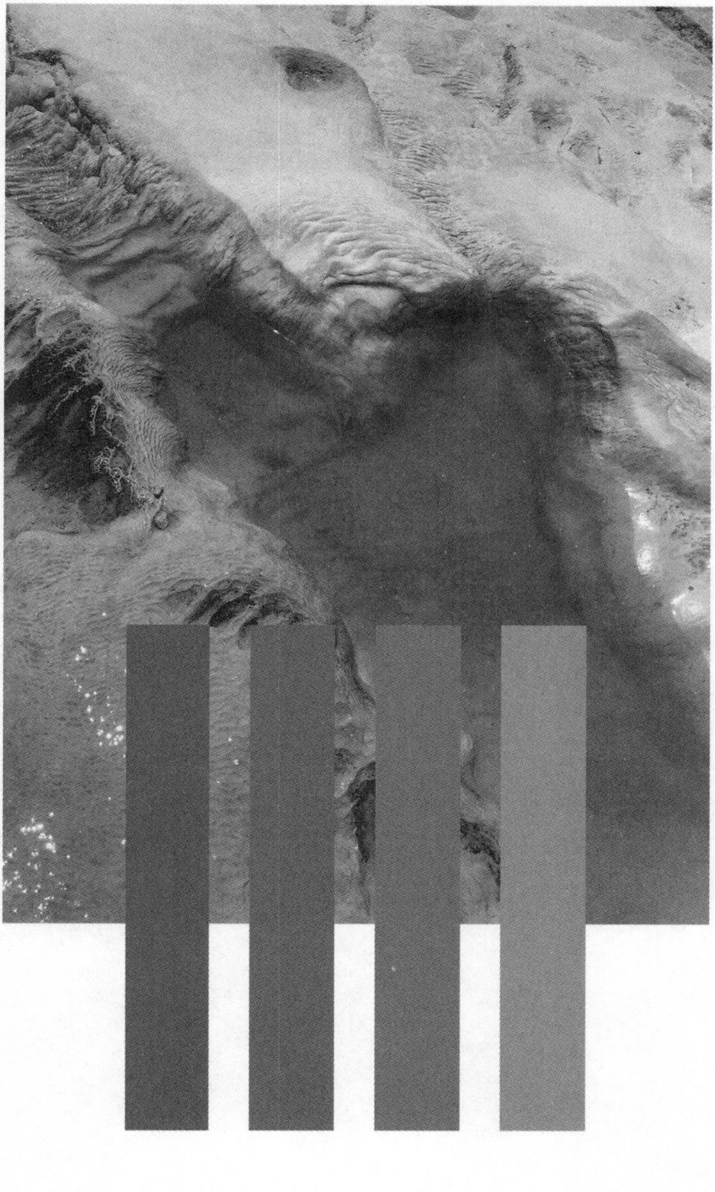

[Several Alternative Terms to Use Instead of Saying Good Father]

A roof / a plane ticket to anywhere / four walls smiling at each other / a car driven at 80 mph / muffled prayers sent to my name / a cobalt-colored safety / raw mangoes from a withering family house / softness[3] / space

[Fragments of Memory]

There's one moon to my name. A lonely cashmere moon. A dying silver-haired moon. A silent eyelash-dropping moon.

The city today is merely the weight of our names. A home of sounds. Everything you said has become a part of my memory. I have a terrible memory. My father is crying in his sleep again.

never, lost or stopped

[Return]

The city is forgetting you / which is to say / you should return home

[When Asked How They Make Art, the Artist Said]

I create when I am [almost] sad / happiness chews my art whole / & throws it away / imagine being in New York with your eyes closed / that would be tragic / imagine creating something out of love / & finding it gone the next morning / the art or the love / what leaves first? / what left first? / I won't make jasmine tea today / I will hide my amethyst rings / a poem has to be written soon / I won't invite happiness tonight

[Lately]

I would break my years into pieces / to find / a small house of mud in agony / some Januarys painted lilac / I can see the home without it disappearing / all the beautiful things still breathing / the neem tree in the backyard / red carnation flowers staining my journals / I have been questioning where do I fit in the holy story? somewhere between the teeth of grief, there's still enough space for us to get out. I say we get out.

[R e m e m b r a n c e]

You were never meant to write or die young. But here we are. I collect words and tear them apart sound by sound. Lock becomes look and look becomes cook and cook becomes ok. Why not?

Our mothers taught us patience and I am still not sure about it. The Moon on your side is friendless. Rose mallows in my garden won't learn to wither. Nothing brings you back now. Not even our songs.

But to let you know, I still listen to that song.

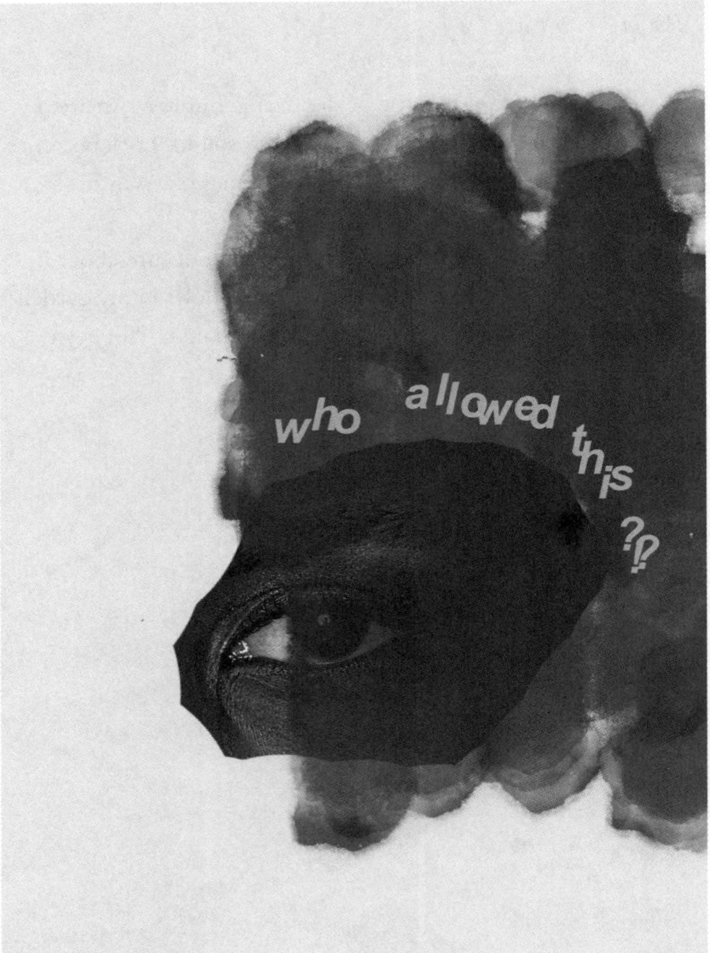
who allowed this ?!?

[Name Your Loneliness]

Here / you name your own loneliness / I have named mine Clementine / we forgot it at a store last night / it grew two legs and ran outside / your loneliness is called Asparagus / none of us ever learned to spell it right / but you do not leave it behind / I keep a pocket dictionary / to name everyone's loneliness right / my mother's—named after roses / my father's—rhymes with flight / if you don't want to name it / call it [a thing to remember] / call it [a purple plastic knife]

[A List of Everything I Want]

The sun / a glass house incapable of breaking / the ashes of a name / some remains of the day / a love wrapped in ancient silver / a sky never turning crimson / a whirling heart / a city naive enough to remember me

FOR MY DUPATTA-WEARING, CASHEW CHEWING.
INDIE POP LISTENING, BOUGAINVILLEA COLLECTING,
OCEAN GAWKING, STARS COUNTING, LAVENDER OIL
HOARDING, GOLD EYEING, HISTORY REPEATING,
GEOMETRIC KURTIS PILING, DRY LEAVES HOLDING,,
AYAT-AL-KURSI RECITING

SELF

MAY YOUR KNUCKLES
FIND ALL THE SILVER AND
MOONSTONE. MAY THE CITIES
OF YOUR DREAMS NEVER DROWN.
MAY YOUR GRIEF FIND A DARK
PINE DOOR AJAR AND LEAVE.
MAY ALL YOUR PRAYERS PIERCE
THROUGH THE HOLY FLESH OF
THE SKY.

[Our Hometowns]

Small—towns. Big, loud, drenched in guiltless blood—towns. Homes stuffed into some hearts—towns. Obedience fit onto billboards—towns. Eating dust for breakfast—towns. Jam-packed with unrequited romance—towns. Painted with whatever you left—towns. You will never be home—towns. Hometowns—some hometowns.

[Our History]

So much of us is past & dust & borders & sound

Suddenly   you are everywhere   even when I'm repelling the moon
            even when I'm flossing my teeth
            even when I'm angry at the shattered lights of my car.
You're here.

I wrote your name backwards and it still looks beautiful
            What has become of me?

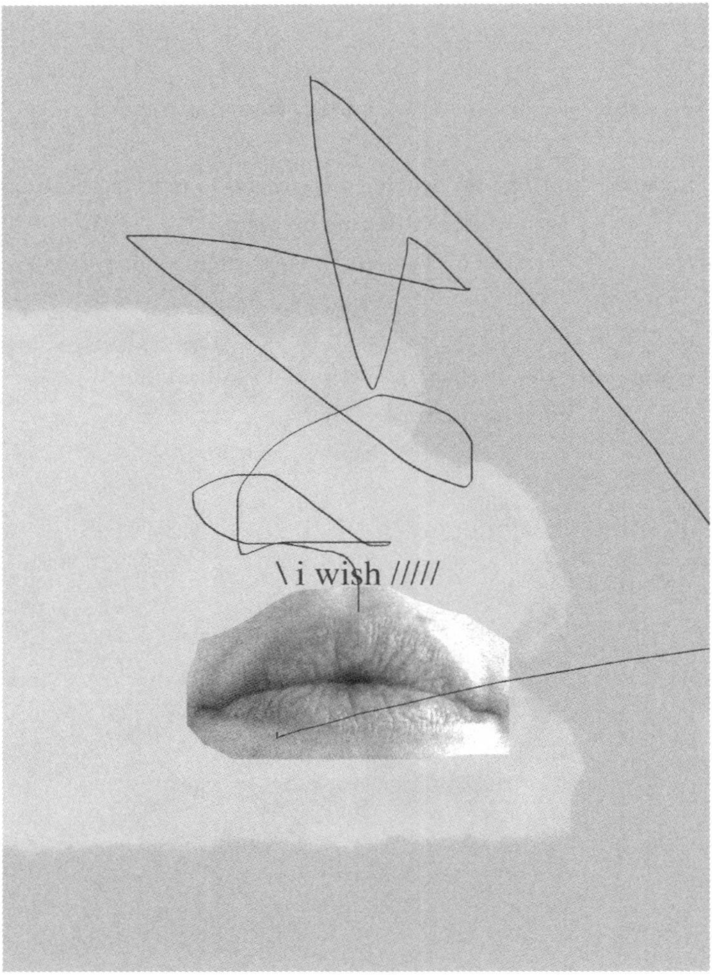
\ i wish /////

[Ms. Loneliness]

My loneliness has a mouth now / it speaks five languages / it collects
dry flowers / & listens to French songs on repeat / it sleeps on time /
restocks the family-sized cereal boxes / has no wifi /

You would
not believe it is mine.

I don't.

[Mood Report]

Synoptic Situation:
Sunset (Wednesday) 17:05 Sunrise (Thursday) 07:04
Sadness is likely to prevail over most parts of the body during next few days.

Past 24 Hours Weather:
Time in my palms wilted unlike roses unlike daisies / I am only a poet when I am crying / you were lucky enough to forget if you did / everything facing me in the room was disappointed / the cracked mason jar / the flickering fairy lights / the black-and-white Polaroids on the wall

Sobbing (mm) During Last 24 Hours:
Nil.

Today's Lowest Minimum Temperatures for Each Feeling:

Loneliness -11°C, Melancholy -07°C, Indifference -05°C, Gratitude -02°C, Rebellion -01°C.

Weather Forecast for Tomorrow:
Mainly, movement and over-speeding is expected in most parts of the day.
Calm is expected in [most] parts of the body.
Shifting apologetic conditions are likely to continue during morning/night hours.

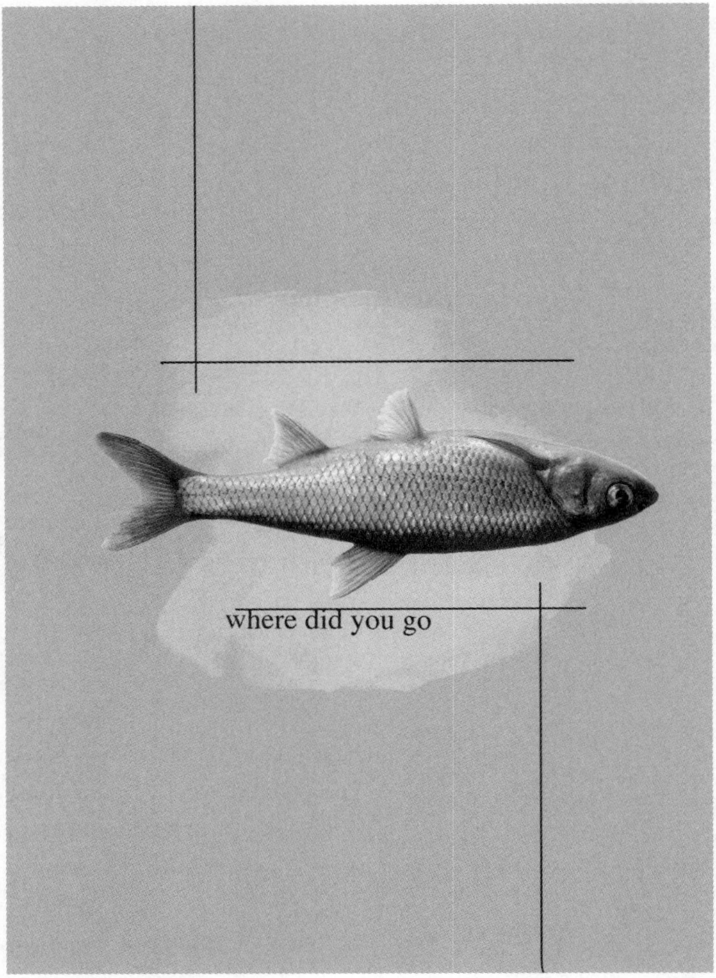
where did you go

[Stargazing]

A number of stars crashed the last time I was stargazing. Glowing bodies dropping dead.
Some said   [ ] that is their end
Some said   they will be born again by the time we see this first act of death

& I prayed

to have my falls as stellar as theirs. To be defeated in the same manner

that by the time the world witnesses my disintegration
I am already light-years away / ready to return as a whole
illuminating body

[History of My Family]

Half of us born in the difficult part of each year / but it was okay / our names taken from all the right things / our women named after stars and other glowing bodies / our men after the great men before them / but that is where it ends / our history was peachy pride wrapped in velvet / rotten but still glorious / I came when the August was aging / all our mango trees were laden with fruit and responsibilities / the [ghost] house of my family is still there / we would go there to remember / we would go there to forget

THE
HU RT
CAM E
FIR ST

THE
HU RT
CAM E
FIR ST

[Part-Everything Daughter]

After Ocean Vuong

I trust water as my mother
trusts Surah Yaseen to protect
me from every satin wolf
outside. Who would I be if not
a cinnamon body
part salt water part everything daughter
born in a city by the sea so generous
it didn't swallow us.
Smoke built a house only to
name it a heart and I swapped
it with the one mourning inside me.
It ignites before it breaks. There
is a God I begged forgiveness from
and was given everything else. If you
ever see me smoldering, assume
I must be apologizing with a heart on
the verge of breaking.

[All the Wrong Things]

I left you back home & in my favorite cities & where the clouds were somehow teal & at the airports & at the shy sunsets & near the horizon & where the asparagus grew & you wouldn't believe but each pomegranate contains a seed from heaven and no it wouldn't grow a heaven if sown here but what is better than that? You'd think I inherited all the wrong things. I didn't. None of my dreams make sound anymore. The sunlight is where it is supposed to be. I left you everywhere so much that nothing looks different and everything reminds me how I carry too little of you now so do you understand the leaving means you'd be in every common noun?

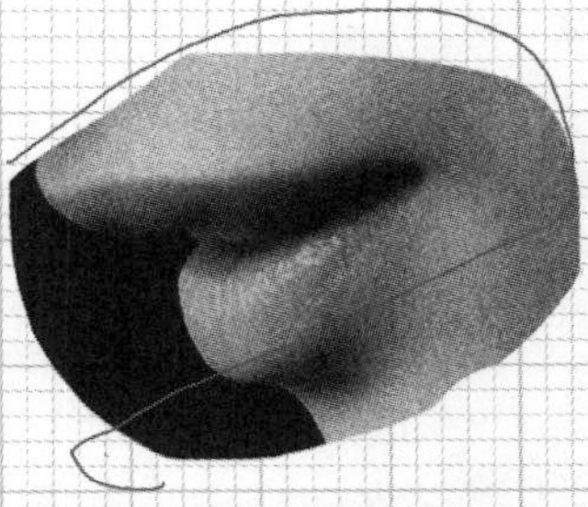

conversations that have nothing

[An Okay Family]

My grandmother left many things
behind. Her gold adorns our necks. My
youngest aunt even has her clothes. We're
a happy family.

My grandmother left her
grief behind. It adorns our dreams. My father inherited
it happily. We might not be a happy family. In my dreams,
more possessions appear. They are silver and they aren't
here. Who forgot them there?

My grandmother died when I was young. I don't
know where her grave is. But when I look at my father,
[at least] I know where her grief is. We might be
an okay family.

[A Twisted Narrative of My Dismay]

We are thrown in this
world with skins borrowed
and hair with histories
entwined in them.
If I weren't me, I would be you.

I want to decide where the
sun could be brighter, unlike
its usual shade of not
listening.
Our weather is more news and less alive.

There is only one sky and
a lot of us. That is a little
shelter when half of it is
taken by unanswered
prayers.
If I were a whisper, I would be about heartbreak
and burning paper.

PEACE
PEACE
PEACE PEACE
PEACE PEACE
PEACE PEACE
PEACE PEACE
PEACE
PEACE

[Protected]

I protect my favorite things by blowing prayers into their flesh
& hope   they go through
the metal of my car   shielded by the names of God
my ambitious sister wrapped   in the velvety verses of   a holy book
the curtains of our room   laced with Surah Ikhlas

[Last Words]

to the father of my father I would say

your sons were born moons / your daughter lilies and strength /
you should have protected them from you / & the anger that
swallowed you whole in the end

[NOTES LEFT FOR A STRANGER AT THE
NAMELESS PARK IN MY HOMETOWN]

COWARDICE IS BRAVERY HALFWAY
            ON A LONG ROAD. I REMEMBER

ALL THE SKIES TOMORROW STOLE
            BUT COUNTING THEM WILL COST
THE LOSS OF ANOTHER ONE.

        WHAT ELSE DO YOU KNOW ABOUT HOME
        BESIDES HOW IT FALLS APART ?

            EVEN FORGIVENESS SOUNDS
LIKE AN AGGRIEVED BLAME
            IN YOUR VOICE.

THERE IS A ROAD TINTED
            WITH EVERYTHING YESTERDAY
LEFT BEHIND. I HAVE BEEN
            SLEEPWALKING ON IT.

[Stuck in History]

Somewhere in this poem, I will shrink back to nothingness. Somewhere, my father would still be a boy who could sing. The mud apple tree in the courtyard of our house will be planted in a few years. My grandmother wants to buy that gold necklace. The garage stairs lead nowhere right now. We were the stars after stars. Aligned. Our lucks rock solid. So much of us is yet to come. So much of us will never will.

[Keeper]

I like to think I can keep things / a tiny dream wrapped in cellophane sheet / two piles of barely used journals / three worn copies of your favorite book / four stones collected from the town my mother grew up in / five seconds of unrequited love / six homes crumbled together by the absence of love / I like to think I can keep things

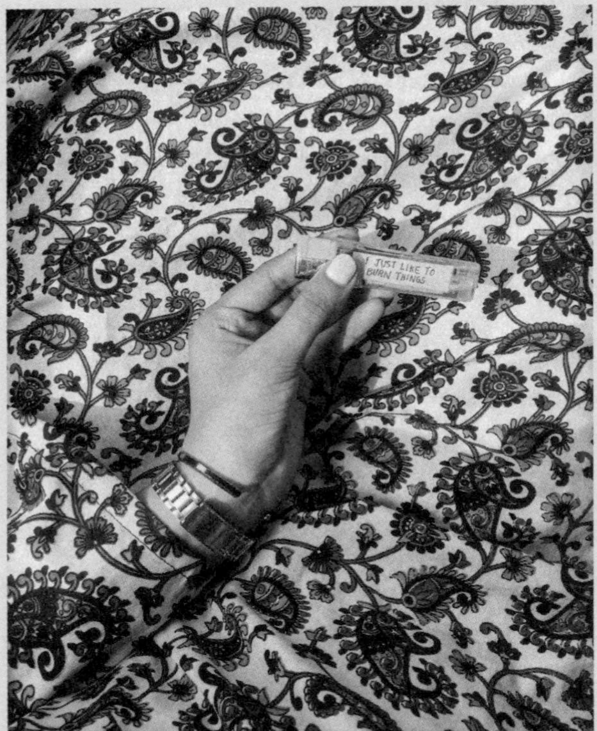
I JUST LIKE TO
BURN THINGS

[Last Day of Summer]

Everything returns home when the summer is dying. You too will leave. I will rescue your leaving in a bad poem. I will gather last summer light in a sad poem.

The clouds are a shade between baby blue and
lilac. The boys are chasing
whatever insects walk slowly. Could we keep a
season on our skies forever? The
God said no. I agree. I would always agree.

It's time to go. Maghrib time marks the end of the day. I mark the end of us. I will see summer next year.

[A Dialogue with Death]

Choose me when you have to. My father is still mad at
you. You took his mother. I would have been mad too.

Take me mid-fall. When the leaves are only half
withered. I will not let flowers mourn me.

I would want to say all the goodbyes. Some of them
set in different time zones. Some just out of my reach.

My history won't leave me. Make it my gleaming
white shroud. It will be okay.

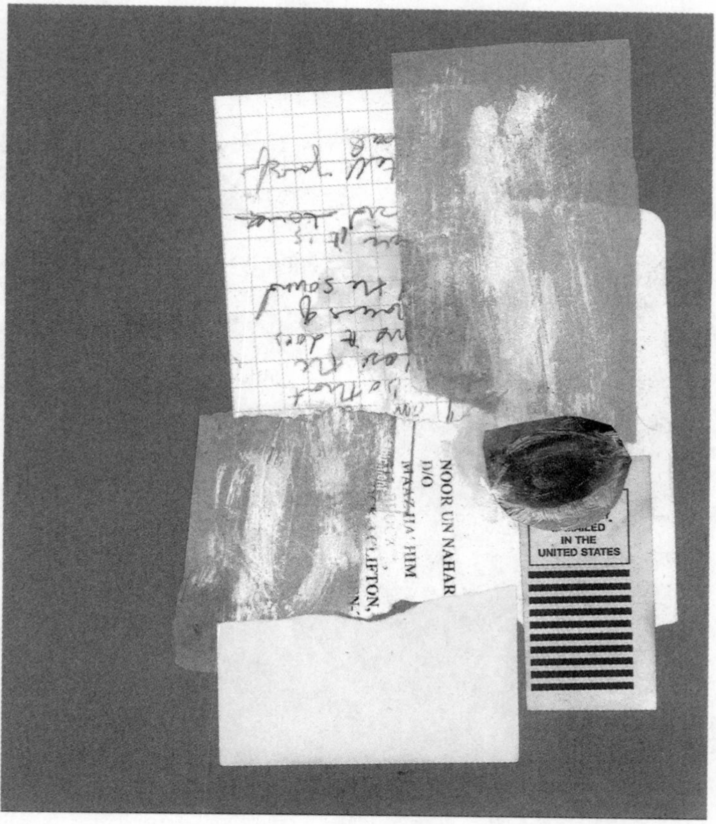
NOOR UN NAHAR
D/O
IN THE
UNITED STATES

[Forget Me Not]

There's very little fear left in me. If we were here,
you wouldn't know me.

I will take protection from my God. I will pray
for what is broken in half.

Love finds you somehow. I am neon lights and gajras.
You are the midnight of New York.

One day we'll forget this together. You could build your
house then. I could leave your town.

[A Non-Worldly Sketch of My Room]

There is more paper
than oxygen in my room /
Yellow, orange, dead
shades of brown;
together we're withering
artistically here.

My mother's suitcase
is still in a corner
but she is fading /
I could have written
my name on it
but I have taken way too
many flights.

The mirror on the wall
is so full of present;
it wouldn't reflect me /
The problem was never
the past—
but the idea of a reluctant
tomorrow.

Come in and have a
look
The air is heavy with
unreleased words /
I wake up every
morning to
distinguish
my voice from all the
other voices.

GLOSSARY

[Pockets] kurti: *a type of tunic or shirt worn especially by women in South Asia, shorter and typically more fitting*

[A Prayer for All of My Selves] dupatta: *a long scarf-like cloth usually worn by women in South Asia*

[Part-Everything Daughter] Surah Yaseen: *Surah Yaseen is the 36th surah of the Quran with 83 verses*

[Winters Named after My Mother] Bismillah: *an Arabic phrase meaning "in the name of God"*

[Winters Named after My Mother] Surah Al-Ikhlas: *another name for Surah Ikhlas, which is the 112th surah of the holy Quran*

[Tonight I Will Have an Easy Name for Dinner] muezzin: *a title for the man who calls Muslims to prayer from a mosque*

[Omens in the History of My Family] Astaghfirullah: *an Arabic phrase meaning "I seek forgiveness in God"*

[Protected] Surah Ikhlas: *Surah Ikhlas is the 112th surah of the holy Quran*

[Last Day of Summer] Maghrib: *the Maghrib prayer is one of the five mandatory Islamic prayers; the period for this prayer starts just after sunset*

[Forget Me Not] gajra: *a flower garland worn by women in South Asia during festive occasions*

new names for lost things

Andrews McMeel Publishing
a division of Andrews McMeel Universal
1130 Walnut Street, Kansas City, Missouri 64106

www.andrewsmcmeel.com

21 22 23 24 25 VEP 10 9 8 7 6 5 4 3 2 1

ISBN: 978-1-5248-6759-1

Library of Congress Control Number:
2021943289

Editor: Allison Adler
Art Director: Tiffany Meairs
Production Editor: Dave Shaw
Production Manager: Cliff Koehler

Cover photo by Davi Moreira